GW00891705

YOUTH BIBLE STUDY GUIDE
Sexuality

Youth Bible Study Guides

Sexuality

Following God

Image and Self-Esteem

Peer Pressure

Father God

Jesus Christ and the Holy Spirit

Sin, Forgiveness and Eternal Life

Church, Prayer and Worship

Sharing Your Faith

Suffering and Depression

Giving

Hunger, Poverty and Justice

YOUTH BIBLE STUDY GUIDE

Sexuality

COMPILED AND WRITTEN BY
CHIP AND HELEN KENDALL

Authentic

First published 2009 by Authentic Media
This revised edition published 2012 by Authentic Media Ltd
Presley Way, Crownhill, Milton Keynes, MK8 0ES.
www.authenticmedia.co.uk

British Library Cataloguing in Publication Data
A catalogue record for this book is available from the British Library

ISBN-13: 978-1-86024-824-5

Extracts taken from:
Trevor Stammers and Tim Doak, *Saving Sex*, Authentic, 2006
Josh McDowell, *Youth Devotions 2*, Tyndale House, 2003
Ems Hancock and Ian Henderson, *Sorted?*, Authentic, 2004
Chip Kendall, *The Mind of Chip K: Enter at Your Own Risk*, Authentic, 2005

Cover and page design by Temple Design
Cover based on a design by Beth Ellis
Printed in Great Britain by Bell and Bain, Glasgow

God wants you to be holy.
He wants you to stay away from sexual sins.
God wants each one of you to learn
to control your own body.
Use your body in a way that is holy
and that gives honour to God.
(1 Thessalonians 4:3,4)

Chip Kendall (formerly of thebandwithnoname) is a singer/songwriter/ communicator who's passionate about modelling something great for this generation. He now spends his time performing live with his amazing band, speaking at events and conferences, leading worship and going into high schools with 'Test of Faith' science weeks to explain the Christian message to teenagers. Chip's first book, *The mind of chipK: Enter at your own risk* has helped loads of young people grow in their faith. Chip is also pioneering a new movement called 'MYvoice' with Cross Rhythms Radio and presents some youth programming for God TV.

www.chipkendall.com

Helen Kendall has spent 10 years working for Innervation Trust as both Team Leader for thebandwithnoname and Assistant Director of the Trust. She now works with their BeBe Vox and Pop Connection projects. Along with writing these study guides Helen has spent time working on the brand new ERV Youth Bible and dancing as part of Manchester-based Allegiance Dance Crew. Helen also makes a mean tray of peanut butter cupcakes which she enjoys eating with Chip and Cole (their son).

Chip and Helen currently live in Stockport, UK.

Thank Yous

First up, thanks to Malcolm Down and all the rest of the team at Authentic for giving us the opportunity to work on these study guides, it's been a blast. To everyone at SFC, who read the books and gave us your thoughts, we appreciate the feedback. Thanks to the lovely Lucy West for the fantastic photos, and Kylie for the typing. To everyone who talked to Chip for the 'people clips', thanks for your honesty and willingness to put up with the quirky questions. A really huge thank you everyone at Audacious City Church for being an amazing church family. Thanks to Brian and Norma Wilson for their 'hidden pearls' of wisdom. We loved your perspective on things. Finally, big thanks to all the authors whose work we have used in this book. You are an inspiration.

CONTENTS

INSTRUCTIONS

The book you're holding in your hands is a study guide. It's a compilation of lots of other books written about this subject. It might not make you the world's expert on the subject, but it should give you lots of useful information and, even better, it should give you some idea of what the Bible has to say about . . . SEXUALITY.

What is a 'reaction box'?

Throughout the book, you'll find these helpful little reaction boxes. We've added them so that you can decide for yourself what you think about what you've just read. Here's what one should look like once you've filled it in:

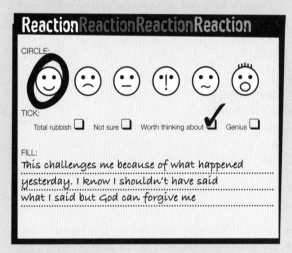

Pretty simple really . . .

Circle the face that reflects how you feel about it.

Tick the box that shows what you think about it.

Fill in any thoughts you have about what you've learned on the lines provided.

What are 'people clips'?

Just so you don't get too bored, we've added a bunch of 'people clips' to each study guide. These are people just like you, who were happy for us to pick their brains about various related topics. Who knows? Maybe you'll find someone you recognize.

What are 'hidden pearls'?

Everyone needs some good old-fashioned 'grandparently' advice, so we collected some pearls of wisdom from our friends Brian and Norma Wilson (aged 86 and 85), which you can find scattered throughout the book.

What is a 'reality check'?

Finally, throughout the book you will come across sections called 'Reality check'. These should provide a chance for you to apply what you've been learning to your own life experiences.

Other than that, the only rule that applies when reading this book is that you HAVE FUN! So start reading.

Chip & Helen

INTRODUCTION
WHAT'S THE BIG DEAL ANYWAY?

Sex *is* a big deal, at least that's the way it seems when you look at the TV, listen to music, check out adverts and magazines or talk to your friends. Sometimes it seems like everything in life is about sex, from finding a partner to buying shampoo! Everyone is doing it, aren't they? In this study guide we are going to try and bring some clarity to the mystery surrounding sex and let you decide whether it really is such a big deal or whether it has been blown out of proportion. We are going to find out what the Bible says about sexuality so that you can make the right decision about when to do it and who with. Make sure you check out the wise words to the lads and ladies on this subject along with the usual hidden pearls of wisdom from the older generation.

We thought it would be interesting to step out of our own shoes and look at the world through the eyes of an alien from outer space. So, we tried to forget all our experiences of life and reality and make assessments about sexuality based only on what we saw on MTV over a 1-hour period.

Alien assumption 1

Women and men must feel temperature differently because all women seem to feel warm most of the time. They seem not to wear very much and still manage to be a bit sweaty! Men on the other hand must feel the cold more, since they wear more clothes.

Alien assumption 2

Most men have many girlfriends or women who want to have sex with them.

Alien assumption 3

Most women are happy to share their men with other women.

As you can see from the slightly crazy assumptions our alien brains came to, music videos don't show what is true in real life. Maybe some people have the kind of lifestyle you see on TV, but most of the women we know certainly aren't happy to share their man with other women! Magazines, music videos and TV glamorize casual sex and make it seem like everyone's doing it. They fail to point out all the negative things such as emotional hurt, STDs and unwanted pregnancy that can accompany sex outside of marriage. We think God definitely knows what's best for you, even more than your school friends, parents or teachers. So let's dig under the surface and find out what the Bible says about . . . SEXUALITY.

What does God say about sex?

The Scriptures say, 'That is why a man will leave his father and mother and join his wife, and the two people will become one.'

(Ephesians 5:31)

First Up

In his Word, the Bible, God has loads to say about sex. God invented sex, he designed us to fancy people, to enjoy snogging, and to want to take it further! He made sex for our enjoyment and for multiplication — babies. In Genesis 1:28 it says,'God blessed them and said to them, "Have many children. Fill the earth and take control of it. Rule over the fish in the sea and the birds in the air. Rule over every living thing that moves on the earth."' Because sex is such a good gift, God has put guidelines around it to protect it and to protect us. This isn't to spoil our fun, but so that we can really enjoy sex instead of settling for a second rate version of it. In this lesson, we will take you through some of the basic ground rules about sex that are laid down by God in the Scriptures to help us enjoy it and not be hurt by it.

Although these days sex is often treated very casually, in Bible times it would be unheard of to have sex before you got married, in fact anyone doing it would be stoned to death if they were caught! When the Bible talks about fornication (not a word we use much today!) or doing indecent things with the body, or immorality, it is clear from the original language that this included sex outside of marriage. Another useful thing to bear in mind as you read the verses below is that since most people will get married at some point in their lives, if you have sex with someone outside of marriage, chances are you are sleeping with someone else's wife/husband.

Check out these Bible verses and see what God says about sex.

Sex outside marriage

But a man who is married is busy with things of the world. He is trying to please his wife. He must think about two things – pleasing his wife and pleasing the Lord. **A woman who is not married or a girl who has never married is busy with the Lord's work. She wants to give herself fully – body and spirit – to the Lord.** But a married woman is busy with things of the world. She is trying to please her husband. I am saying this to help you. I am not trying to limit you, but I want you to live in the right way. And I want you to give yourselves fully to the Lord without giving your time to other things.

(1 Corinthians 7:33–35, emphasis added)

Desire

Brothers and sisters, now I have some other things to tell you. We taught you how to live in a way that will please God. And you are living that way. Now we ask and encourage you in the Lord Jesus to live that way more and more. You know all that we told you to do by the authority of the Lord Jesus. **God wants you to be holy. He wants you to stay away from sexual sins. God wants each one of you to learn to control your own body. Use your body in a way that is holy and that gives honour to God. Don't let your sexual desires control you** like the people who don't know God.

(1 Thessalonians 4:1–5, emphasis added)

Thought life

But I tell you that if a man looks at a woman and wants to sin sexually with her, he has already committed that sin with her in his mind. If your right eye makes you sin, take it out and throw it away. It is better to lose one part of your body than to have your whole body thrown into hell.

(Matthew 5:28,29, emphasis added)

Honouring God

'I am allowed to do anything,' you say. My answer to this is that **not all things are good.** Even if it is true that 'I am allowed to do anything', **I will not let anything control me like a slave.** Someone else says, 'Food is for the stomach, and the stomach for food.' Yes, and God will destroy them both. But **the body is not for sexual sin. The body is for the Lord and the Lord is for the body.** And God will raise our bodies from death with the same power he used to raise the Lord Jesus.

(1 Corinthians 6:12–14, emphasis added)

Sinning against your body

Surely you know that your bodies are parts of Christ himself. So I must never take what is part of Christ and join it to a prostitute!
The Scriptures say, **'The two people will become one.' So you should know that anyone who is joined with a prostitute becomes one with her in body.** But anyone who is joined with the Lord is one with him in spirit.

So run away from sexual sin. It involves the body in a way that no other sin does. So if you commit sexual sin, you are sinning against your own body. You should know that your body is a temple for the Holy Spirit that you received from God and that lives in you. You don't own yourselves. God paid a high price to make you his. So honour God with your body.

(1 Corinthians 6:15–20, emphasis added)

Virginity

Virginity is very important for Christians. Christ himself, though no sexual prude, never married and was a virgin, despite suggestions to the contrary of popular fiction such as *The Da Vinci Code* by Dan Brown (Bantam Press, 2003). Jesus also spoke of those who choose a lifelong state of virginity in order to give priority to serving God without distraction (Matthew 19:12). Sex can certainly still be a major distraction in that regard today and we should applaud and support rather than ridicule those who make a deliberate choice to avoid sexual involvement in their teens and twenties in order to devote their lives to Christian work which otherwise could not be done.

For those who eventually marry, the expectation of the New Testament is that they should be virgins when they do so (1 Corinthians 7:33–35). Though there is no scripture that specifically states 'no sex outside of marriage' the Greek word *pornea* (translated sexual immorality or fornication) clearly includes sex outside of marriage in its meaning and is forbidden in many parts of the New Testament (1 Corinthians 6:18; Ephesians 5:3,4; Colossians 3:5,6; 1 Thessalonians 4:3–5; Hebrews 12:16; 1 Peter 4:3).

Why this seemingly restrictive teaching? The key reason is that sexual intercourse always has a spiritual component; even what we might consider to be the most casual of sexual encounters, e.g. that between a prostitute and her client, has this element. 'The Scriptures say, "The two people will become one." So you should know that anyone who is joined with a prostitute becomes one with her in body' (1 Corinthians 6:16). **HAVING SEX WITH SOMEONE FORMS A SPIRITUAL BOND BETWEEN YOU THAT CAN NEVER BE UNDONE.** This is why sex for the first time is a crucial milestone in life. You can never be the same again. Sex is at its best in a loving, committed relationship and if first sex is to be the best sex, it is worth saving it until marriage.

Trevor Stammers and Tim Doak, *Saving Sex*, Authentic, 2006

ReactionReactionReactionReaction

CIRCLE:

TICK:

Total rubbish ☐   Not sure ☐   Worth thinking about ☐   Genius ☐

FILL:

....
....
....
....
....

Sex isn't a dirty word

Bible reading: Song of Songs 4:8–11

'My bride, my dearest, you have stolen my heart
with just one look from your eyes.'

(Song of Songs 4:9)

Reruns of the TV show *Saturday Night Live* show comedian Dana Carvey playing a comically prudish character called the Church Lady. The attitude of this old lady in her long dress and pulled-back hair is a perfect picture of how some people see Christians. They think the followers of Jesus believe in a God who condemns sex and sexuality. Not true.

S ex isn't a dirty word to God. Or even to ladies at church. It's not wrong, sinful or shameful. God doesn't hate sex. He's the one who invented it! He started the whole thing. Sex has been part of God's plan from the beginning (see Genesis 1:27–31). When he told humans, 'Fill the earth' (verse 28), he meant for them to obey him through the activity of procreation, or sex.

The Bible contains some frank accounts of sexuality. The Song of Songs, of course, is a love poem with language that would shock the Church Lady. The apostle Paul offered down-to-earth advice on sexual behaviour to married couples in the church at Corinth. And Scripture doesn't try to hide the fact that sex is to be enjoyed between husband and wife (see Hebrews 13:4).

God created sex. It is *humans* who have taken it outside the marriage covenant and dirtied it. God meant sex to be a fulfilling, exciting, satisfying experience between a man and woman totally surrendered to each other in the enjoyment of each other's sexuality. It is *people* who have perverted God's gift.

When God tells you not to commit adultery or not to have anything to do with sexual immorality, he doesn't do it to wreck your life.

God wants to **protect** you from distrust or suspicion and provide for you one of the most important factors for a fulfilled marriage and sexual relationship: trust.

God wants to **shield** you from the fear of sexually transmitted diseases and to provide peace of mind when you enter into marriage.

God wants to **shelter** you from bad relationships that are artificially sustained by sexual involvement – the kind that often lead to tragic marriages.

God wants to **protect** your virginity, one of the greatest gifts a person can present to a mate on his or her wedding night.

Can you believe God loves you that much? It's true. He's not trying to spoil your fun. He's trying to show you the way to real fun.

Josh McDowell, *Youth Devotions 2*, Tyndale House, 2003

ReactionReactionReactionReaction

CIRCLE:

TICK:

Total rubbish ☐   Not sure ☐   Worth thinking about ☐   Genius ☐

FILL:

....

....

....

....

....

The Spirit of Sex

Bible Reading: 1 Corinthians 6:15–20

The Scriptures say, 'The two people will become one.'
(1 Corinthians 6:16)

Want to know the secret of the world's best sex? The Bible points out that a husband and wife become 'one' (Genesis 2:24). And here's the secret: the best sex comes in marriage – and after a deep, spiritual relationship has been established.

S ex can affect you in almost the same way knowing God does. God knows you all the way to your innermost being – and he loves you in spite of your faults. Having sex with someone means you reveal yourself at a truly deep level – and not just physically. Sex makes you both more humble and more secure, because you realize your husband or wife loves you in spite of any faults he or she finds in you. And the closer a husband and wife grow spiritually, the more they enjoy their sex life. God blesses sex in a spiritual way and uses it to build up a married couple emotionally.

See it? You get to expect more from sex than the physical. Humans aren't like animals. Ever noticed a female dog in heat and the male dogs around her? It is obvious that the sexual behaviour of dogs is purely animal instinct.

For humans, sex involves your mind – your ability to choose. And because your mind and spirit are constantly involved – as are your emotions – sex is always very personal. The relationship between a man and woman is never the same as it was before they had sex. After having sex and then breaking up, many people confess that they feel like they left a part of their self with another person. And they really did. That's what the Bible means when it says that through sex a man and woman become 'one'.

Someday when the time comes to give yourself to your husband or wife, that person will know something about you he or she can never forget. And you will know him or her in the same way. In fact, that word 'know' is the word some translations of the Bible use to describe the sex act, as in Genesis 4:1: 'Adam knew his wife' (KJV). Did you know that?

God made sex to be a way a husband and wife say something incredibly special to each other. Every time a married couple shares sex together, they celebrate the vows they made on their wedding day and the oneness they have on all levels – spiritually, mentally, and emotionally as well as physically. As you walk close with Jesus and he leads you in his time to the person with whom you will share all of yourself you will be able to have every bit of this and even more.

Josh McDowell, *Youth Devotions 2*, **Tyndale House, 2003**

ReactionReactionReactionReaction

CIRCLE:

TICK:

Total rubbish ☐   Not sure ☐   Worth thinking about ☐   Genius ☐

FILL:

....

....

....

....

....

Relationships

Animals have sex to procreate to make babies. They don't have sex because they love each other, or for a laugh or because they have had too much to drink! We do. Animals don't fall in love or cry when they get dumped. We do. We are different from animals. There is something in us that wants to know more than sex. We want to know that we are accepted. We want to be liked. We want to be loved. That's how God made us. He designed us to want relationships. Not so very long ago, people were given a lot of help from family and friends with 'courting' (going out) and marriage. Now, of course, going out with someone is totally private and sometimes even secret. The pressure is on us to find a partner. So if and when we get the opportunity, what sort of person should we go out with?

Ems Hancock and Ian Henderson, *Sorted?*, Authentic, 2004

2

First up

OK. Let's go back to the very beginning.
Read Genesis 1:24–28.

Are you finished?
Now do your best to answer some of these questions.

What order did God make animals and people in?

What is the biggest difference between animals and people?

(Clue: check out verse 27.)

Throughout the Bible we see that God loves relationships. After creating Adam and Eve he walked with them in the garden of Eden (read Genesis 3:8). If we are made in God's image, then what does this say about us?

(Clue: read Genesis 2:18.)

God clearly made us to have relationships, but these don't necessarily have to be boyfriend/girlfriend relationships, or even sexual relationships. Check out what this next section has to say about singleness and dating. These are some wise words!

Single and lovin' it

I'm dying for a snog

Mostly, being single doesn't feel too good, does it? Sure, loads of people (even celebs) might not have a boy/girlfriend, but they play the field, taking advantage of 'not being tied down'. But if you are a Christian, you know that you can't just get off with loads of people and be a 'player' (if you're not sure why we'll cover that later). **SO FOR YOU, BEING SINGLE MEANS NO SNOGS, NO SEX, NOTHING!** You may have heard people say that sex is an appetite, you have to fulfil it. 'If you're thirsty you drink – if you're feeling sexy, sleep with someone.' Only thing is, you can die from not drinking. We've never heard of anyone dying from not having sex or lack of snogging! You *can* survive being single!

I don't want to be alone

GOD DOESN'T INTEND FOR ANYONE TO BE *ALONE*. He made us all with the desire and need to be part of other people's lives. But there are some people who will always be single. We know that Jesus had close friendships with people around him; he didn't 'need' a girlfriend and didn't get married. He chose this way of life. Jesus was single; he didn't see it as a second-best option.

There are some people for whom singleness is the only choice. Maybe they have never fallen in love, or perhaps they have loved someone who was not available. Others have chosen to be celibate because they are gay. For others, they lead fulfilling lives without the need to be 'completed' by another person.

Our society gives singleness a bad press. But God sees it differently. For some people singleness is exactly what he wants for them. He knows it is right for their lives and that they can do all and be all he called them to be as a single person. 1 Corinthians 7:32–34 talks about how those who are not married can be dedicated to God in a way that married people may not be. So don't discount it. It is the best thing for certain people. (You may want to check out Matthew 19:12 too.)

You might be thinking, 'Hang on, I'm not worried about getting married, I just want to go out with someone.' There's an old saying: 'The moment you stop trying to meet someone, you'll meet them.' Sometimes that can seem true, but what is true is that the moment you start enjoying having great mates around you, having a laugh without having 'someone', trusting God for your future, single or not, the happier you will become – whether you are single for a few months or decades. Our single friends (however old they are) are normal, attractive, intelligent, godly, kind and fun. They are not 'sad' or 'losers'. They're just not 'with someone'. Many might believe that it is better to wait for Mr/Mrs Right and won't settle for Mr/Mrs Right Now. They might believe that it is better never to marry than to marry the wrong person! But as we have already said, others believe they are in God's perfect will and are trusting him with the future – whether that future includes a life partner or not.

Ems Hancock and Ian Henderson, *Sorted?*, Authentic, 2004

ReactionReactionReactionReaction

CIRCLE:

☺ ☹ 😐 😯 🙂 😮

TICK:

Total rubbish ☐ Not sure ☐ Worth thinking about ☐ Genius ☐

FILL:

....

....

....

....

....

In the following extract from *The Mind of ChipK*, Chip talks about contentment. He uses a story about not having enough food, but see if you can apply this to the idea of finding contentment with singleness.

Contentment

chipK's mind

When I was growing up in Jerusalem, things weren't always peachy. Being an American teenager with an American appetite stuck in a Middle Eastern world of veggie salads and kosher meat, proved to be quite difficult at times. I'd gone from 'dessert' food to 'desert' food and, trust me, I was gagging for that missing 's'.

M y parents, my sister and I firmly believed that God had called us to live by faith, so we moved to Jerusalem with no promise of a pay cheque for my dad, just a bunch of friends and family pledging support from 'the land of plenty' back home.

I remember one evening our cupboards were literally bare. At the dinner table Mom asked us, 'Have you heard of the Last Supper?' 'Yes,' we all replied. 'Well, you're eating it!' Miraculously, a bit of dosh arrived the next day from one of our supporters who said she'd had a dream that we'd run out of food and wound up eating 'bug sandwiches'. That money covered our next day's food budget, so thankfully the dream never came true!

That was an extreme example of a missionary family learning to trust God to provide their needs. But I think it was also a good lesson in contentment. To be honest with you, I'm still learning that same lesson. I'm faced with situations every day when I have to decide between complaining or choosing to be content. Am I going to groan, or am I going to grow? A great way to battle the moan of what you ain't got is to remind yourself of what you do got.

God's mind

I am telling you this, but not because I need something. I have learned to be satisfied with what I have and with whatever happens. I know how to live when I am poor and when I have plenty. I have learned the secret of how to live through any kind of situation - when I have enough to eat or when I am hungry, when I have everything I need or when I have nothing. Christ is the one who gives me the strength I need to do whatever I must do.
(Philippians 4:11–13)

Do everything without complaining or arguing. Then you will be free from blame and pure, children of God without any fault. But you are living with evil people all around you, who have lost their sense of what is right. Among those people you shine like lights in a dark world, and you offer them the teaching that gives life. So I can be proud of you when Christ comes again. You will show that my work was not wasted - that I ran in the race and won.
(Philippians 2:14–16)

Give us the food we need for today.
(Matthew 6:11)

Your mind

One thing I wish I had, but I don't:

Three things I've got that I'm thankful for:

1.

2.

3.

What do I complain the most about?

Why is it easier to groan than it is to grow?

Chip Kendall, *The Mind Of ChipK: Enter At Your Own Risk*, Authentic, 2005

ReactionReactionReactionReaction

CIRCLE:

☺ ☹ 😐 😲 😕 😮

TICK:

Total rubbish ☐   Not sure ☐   Worth thinking about ☐   Genius ☐

FILL:

....
....
....
....
....

Hidden pearls

'We started dating at about 14. Dating, as long
as it's kept within reason is OK. It's good to
get to know people like that.'

The dating game

So maybe you are already in a relationship. Here are a few extracts that talk about some of the challenges you might face.

What's the latitude of your dating attitude?

Bible reading: Philippians 2:1–4

> Don't be interested only in your own life, but care about the lives of others too.

(Philippians 2:4)

Did Noah ever take his future bride on a romantic boat ride? Did Moses ever take his girlfriend to the Saturday night chariot races? Did Jacob and Rachel go out for pizza and Cokes before they were married? Did Solomon ever take any of his 700 wives and 300 concubines on a date? You might never know the answers to those deep dating questions, because you can't find dating in the Bible – for the same reason you can't find Sunday school. Sunday school and dating weren't part of Bible-times society. Back then, most marriages were prearranged by parents (see Genesis 24 for example).

Just think about how great ready-made marriages would be. No worries about finding a partner. No problem about locating a date for the prom. No more demands from your friends to go out with some loser. No more dateless weekends. Your biggest worry would be figuring out who to double with.

The arranged-marriage plan has drawbacks, however. Your parents might do a deal for you to marry the cutest baby on the block – but in high school he might still be sucking his thumb. Then there's that little thing called love – which most of us want to find *before* we marry. And your parents can't even pick out clothes you like, so how could they pick out a husband or wife you would like? Given those alternatives, you're probably glad for today's system of dating.

Although you can't find dating in the Bible, you can find plenty of Scripture verses that apply to your dating relationships. Most of them have to do with attitudes. Some people enter dating with an attitude of *ownership*. **THEY THINK YOU BELONG TO THEM** and refuse to allow you to live your own life. They act as if you are their private property and want you to fulfil their every whim.

Then there are those who approach dating with an attitude of *relationship*. They put all the emphasis on being 'in love'. They major on the romantic and go ugly with insecurity and jealousy when you go out with another person. Philippians 2:3,4 expresses the right attitude to have about dating: *friendship*. The purpose of dating isn't to meet *your* needs but the other person's needs. It isn't to 'fall in love' but to grow in friendship. A relationship rooted in friendship is God's idea of the appropriate attitude for any two people to have. And that includes two people who are dating.

Josh McDowell, *Youth Devotions 2*, Tyndale House, 2003

ReactionReactionReactionReaction

CIRCLE:

TICK:

Total rubbish ☐   Not sure ☐   Worth thinking about ☐   Genius ☐

FILL:

....

....

....

....

....

Name: **Rosie Simmonds**

Age: **15**

Town: **Southend-on-Sea, Essex**

Current status: **Preparing to do GCSEs**

Have you ever dated anyone?

Yes.

What was the experience like?

I've had two very long relationships at a very young age. It was independent of God.

What would you say to someone who's in that place right now, and they need to get out?

They should pray to God for help, because that's what I did. He'll sort it out for you. That's what he did for me.

Reality Check

THE DATING QUIZ

Take this little quiz to find out what your dating habits say about you.

You just split up with your boyfriend/girlfriend and a new, hot lad/lass shows up in youth group. Do you

   a leave him/her in no doubt that you quite fancy him/her and are available?

   b try to get him/her on his/her own so you can find out more about them?

   c chat to him/her as part of a group but not rush into anything?

You are having a youth group social and going out to the cinema. Do you

   a get dressed up to the nines – socials are your time to dress to impress?

   b call your friends and ask what they are wearing and then dress to fit in?

   c head out in whatever you are wearing, you are all just friends, it's not a big deal?

How do you act around the opposite sex?

   a Somehow something flirty always slips out.

   b Go all red and don't really know what to say.

   c Treat them just like you would treat your same sex friends.

Which of the following describes you?

a Always have a boyfriend/girlfriend.

b Never had a boyfriend/girlfriend.

c Have lots of good friends who are boys and girls but only occasionally date exclusively.

If God told you tomorrow that he wanted you to be single for the next 5 years, what would you think?

a It's the end of the world! What am I supposed to do without a boyfriend/girlfriend?

b Well I never date anyone anyway, so what's the big deal?

c It's a hard challenge but I might enjoy not having to worry about finding a partner.

ANALYSIS

If you mostly answered 'a'

You are obviously an outgoing friendly person which is great. God made you like that. However, if you always find yourself flirting, trying to impress or needing a partner, maybe you aren't very secure in who you are. Remember, God loves you, just you, just the way you are. You don't need a boy/girlfriend to define you or give you meaning or value. We would challenge you to take a break from dating for a while, maybe for 6 months or a year. Take some time to find out what God says about you and don't worry about what people say. Psalm 139:14 says, 'I praise you because you made me in such a wonderful way. I know how amazing that was!' He made you wonderful and thinks you are fantastic.

If you mostly answered 'b'

It seems that you might struggle with shyness or lack of confidence. You find it hard to interact with the opposite sex and don't really know what to say to them. This can be really hard but we would encourage you to be yourself. Be secure in the fact that God loves you and thinks you are great, probably most people do, too. Try to relax around members of the opposite sex and just get to know them as friends. Once you've done this you will feel much more comfortable and able to chat. Relationships that start from good friendships are always the ones that last the longest, so focus on making friends rather than worrying about getting a boy/girlfriend. You could discuss how you're feeling with a trusted friend and get them to pray with you about it. If you've never dated anyone before don't worry, we know lots of people who only dated the one person they ended up marrying and this saved them a lot of heartache. God made you just the way you are and he has the perfect partner for you. He will bring it all together in his perfect timing.

If you mostly answered 'c'

You seem to be fairly well balanced about dating and the opposite sex. You are content to just be friends and hang out with a group of people rather than feeling you need to have an exclusive relationship all the time. Keep it up. When you do meet someone you'd like to date, make sure you still maintain the friendships you have with other people and still go out in groups of people.

LIFE LESSON THREE

Why wait?

God wants each one of you to learn to control your own body. Use your body in a way that is holy and that gives honour to God.

1 Thessalonians 4:4

3

First up

Everyone else is doing it, so why can't you? You know the Bible says you should keep sex for inside marriage but it just seems like such an old fashioned idea in today's society. It's totally unrealistic and proves that God is just out to spoil your fun . . . Right? Not really.

Despite the fact that most non-Christians think it is total madness to save sex for marriage, there are actually tons of reasons why it's better to wait. First of all, as we discovered earlier, God said it. And since he created you (along with the rest of the world) he might just know what is best for you. Secondly, by keeping sex inside of marriage you save yourself loads of hurt, risk and hassle and guarantee that once you get to have sex, it will be a great experience, instead of a potentially dodgy one.

Both of us did it God's way and waited until we were married to have sex. This meant that we didn't have to worry about sexually transmitted diseases picked up from previous relationships, we didn't have deep ties to other people, and we didn't have to work through loads of jealousy and comparisons with previous partners. Some people might say that we missed out on getting more experience before we were married, or that you should 'try before you buy'. We think that by waiting until we were married, we saved the best till last and made sure we got everything God planned for us, his way.

Some people say, 'But we're going to get married anyway, so why wait?' We would say, what's the big hurry then? If you are sure you will get married then you probably have 50 years to have sex after the wedding day so why rush into it now, it's not like you are going to miss your chance? What you will never have again is this time of dating or engagement – it's time limited, so take advantage of it while you can. There may be times later in life when you wish you could go back to the carefree times when you were dating. Make the most of each phase while you are in it instead of rushing on to the next one.

Check out what the Bible says in Ecclesiastes 3:1–8.

Finished? Now, write down what the second half of verse 5 says:

Ready for sex?

S ex is seen as a status symbol, as something adult and exciting. But wanting sex doesn't mean we are ready for it. In Britain, we are legally allowed to have sexual intercourse with someone of the opposite sex at the age of sixteen. However, at this age we are considered too young to drive a car, to buy alcohol, to have a credit card or to vote! It may be good to remember that whilst we may have the **physical ability** to have a sexual relationship, the **psychological ability** to be a mature and committed and loving partner takes quite a bit of work! In school we learn about '*safer sex*' – using condoms and contraception to protect ourselves from unwanted pregnancy and sexually transmitted diseases. But God wants us to enjoy totally safe sex not just safer sex.

God knows that it's more than just our bodies that need protecting once we start having sex. **SEX IS DANGEROUS**. The intimacy of sex makes us emotionally, physically and spiritually vulnerable with our partner. We need someone we can totally love and trust for the rest of our lives to be completely safe.

For several decades, society has 'enjoyed' sex without the 'restrictions' of God's way of doing things. But God gave us those restrictions not to trap us but to protect us. Like the safety bar on a roller coaster that restricts and holds you back so you don't fall out! God knows what he is doing. Since society has done what 'feels good', adultery, divorce, teenage pregnancy, abortion, STDs, Aids and child abuse have all increased.

Ems Hancock and Ian Henderson, *Sorted?*, Authentic, 2004

ReactionReactionReactionReaction

CIRCLE:

TICK:

Total rubbish ☐   Not sure ☐   Worth thinking about ☐   Genius ☐

FILL:

....

....

....

What if you're in a loving relationship?

> I'm in a relationship at the moment and we both really love each other. We've talked about having sex and think it would be a good idea but how can we really be sure?

It sounds to me like you have a good relationship in which you can talk about this very important issue. I'm sure you feel a great deal for each other. If you have such a great relationship, do you really want to jeopardize it by having sex? Often when sex enters into teenage relationships, the relationship soon ends. I can't be absolutely sure why this is, but I know that when a couple in their early to mid-teens start to have sex, other more important aspects of their relationship, like friendship, are often forgotten, because they tend to focus too much just on the physical side.

I know your feelings are really strong and it's perfectly natural to want to have sex, but you have to decide whether it's going to be worth it and what you want for your life, not only now but in the future as well. Think of the possible consequences: you could get pregnant; you could pick up an STD; you could risk jeopardizing a great relationship. How will you feel emotionally if you split up and you've lost your virginity? These are all things you have to think through seriously before you make any decisions.

You may be or think that you are in love, but is that enough? **THE AVERAGE PERSON FALLS IN LOVE SEVEN TIMES IN THEIR LIFE**, though for some it is more like seven times a week! Imagine the consequences if you slept with everyone you fell in love with. I hope you don't think I'm trying to spoil your fun because the choice is yours and I'm not trying to take that away from you. But I don't want you to have regrets in the future or put your health at risk. Be sure – there's a lot at stake.

Trevor Stammers and Tim Doak, *Saving Sex*, Authentic, 2006

ReactionReactionReactionReaction

CIRCLE:

😊 ☹️ 😐 😮 😌 😲

TICK:

Total rubbish ☐   Not sure ☐   Worth thinking about ☐   Genius ☐

FILL:

....
....
....
....
....

Practical reasons to wait

Helen talks

STDs

Now if you ever wanted a good reason to wait to have sex, here is a biggie and it's spelt S T D. Even aside from all the spiritual and biblical reasons to wait until marriage to have sex, avoiding one of these yuckies should be more than enough reason. Having sex with anyone, unless you are both virgins, means you are at risk of catching a sexually transmitted disease or infection (STD or STI). STDs are a nasty bunch with symptoms ranging from lice and warts (and I don't mean on your head or hands) to infertility and even death. All STDs are painful and embarrassing and highly infectious. Sometimes symptoms don't show up for years, so someone with an STD could have passed it on to loads of others without even knowing they had it. We know this all sounds very heavy, but the more sexual partners you have, the more likely you are to pick something up that could affect you, your future partner and even your children for the rest of your lives. Chlamydia is now the most commonly reported STD in the UK with **10% TO 15% OF WOMEN IN CERTAIN CITIES INFECTED**. Diagnoses of Chlamydia in the UK increased by 207% between 1996 and 2005 which means that the chances of catching it just keep getting higher.

Some of these infections, especially pubic lice and scabies can be caught without even having full on sex, just being all over each other will do it! Some can be prevented by the use of condoms but ultimately the only way to be 'safe' is to wait until you have found the one person you want to be with for ever and have sex with only them.

Unwanted pregnancy

The other major possible side effect of sex is pregnancy! God made sex to create babies and even if you are very careful you could create one without meaning to, or being ready for it. I have been married to Chip for nearly 7 years and I've just found out that I am pregnant. I'm really excited but also kind of nervous because I know my life is going to change forever. I've got all these questions running round my head like: What should I eat? When should we tell people? How long can I keep dancing? What will it be like to have a baby? I am very glad that I don't have questions like: Who is the father? How will I tell my parents? What will my boyfriend think? Where will I live? also going through my head. Chip is also thinking about how he will look after the baby: Will he be able to provide enough money? Will he be able to support me? It will mean a lot of changes for him, too.

PREGNANCY IS A HUGE THING TO DEAL WITH even if you are in a secure relationship and are ready for it. God knew that all babies deserve to be brought up in the best environment possible by people who love each other, who love the baby and who have a marriage commitment to stay together. This is why he tells us to wait till marriage to have sex. Getting pregnant when you are a teenager can be very scary. Here's the story of a friend of mine who got pregnant by accident at 18 years old.

Whitney's story

'When I found out that I was pregnant, I was really scared. I was scared because I knew I had to tell my parents, I knew it was wrong and that God was not pleased with me and the sinful life I carried. But then it was hard because the guy I was with wanted to have a baby and he seemed excited – so I had to seem like I was, too, when I was around him but really deep down I was scared to death. Since having my son, my life is totally changed. The second I found out that I was pregnant I re-evaluated everything in my life. I thought about who my friends were – because that would influence the baby – I changed the type of music I listened to, the things I said, my actions, my selfish thinking, everything. Through being pregnant, I was being forced to grow up and take on responsibility. Before I had the baby, I had no expenses. My parents bought me food, and really, anything I needed they took care of. Now that it's me and my son, I work full time, I pay for our food, my car payment, insurance, and gas. My parents have helped out when I needed them to but my way of thinking has changed, as far as taking on this responsibility and being a mom.

'My life compared to my friends who have not had babies is completely different. Before I had Blake (my son), my friends were just partying and "livin' it up" without a care in the world. Now, they are going to university full time and working and trying to start their careers. Their main focus is university, when mine is trying to go to university but more than that, trying to work full time, as well as university full time, as well as paying off bills and taking care of a one-and-a-half-year-old boy. It's hard, and they can stay up late when I need to go home early for my son to get to bed. I used to pull those all-nighters but can't anymore. It's hard to hang out with them and do group things because I can't take Blake half of the time, e.g.

movies, playing volleyball (he is scared of the sand). I can't stay long when we're just hanging out at someone's house – he will get bored and get into things. So it's hard for me to have a social life, but they can do that. It's also hard to relate to them when they have never had to go through this, yet they support me and tell me how much they admire me and how they couldn't do it if it were them, so that is encouraging. I guess the big difference between my friends and me is that I can't do everything they can do, and sometimes it just appears that I'm excluding myself from "the group", when really it's just too hard or I'm just too tired. It's hard to explain that to people who can't relate.'

Here is Whitney's advice to teenagers who want to have a baby, or who think they might be pregnant.

'The advice I would give to a teenager wanting to have a baby, but not yet pregnant, is first to question: why? Since I have had a baby, a lot of old high school friends have called me saying they want to have a baby, or are pregnant and ask for my opinion and advice. What I have found is that a lot of girls want to get pregnant so their boyfriend won't leave them . . . or basically so people would feel sorry for them. I would explain to them how it's not as easy as it may look. Even married people who have two incomes wait to have babies because it is so expensive, let alone a single mom. Having a baby won't necessarily mean your boyfriend will stay with you – babies cause a lot of complications in marriages and even more so in dating relationships. Most people who are not married, and are still with their boyfriend and have a baby, still feel alone. For someone who thinks they might be pregnant, I would tell them that it's too late to do anything now. Right now, they just need to pray and trust in God. They need to change their ways and not put themselves in vulnerable positions. I would explain that even taking that "morning after pill" is a way of abortion and if they were wanting to go down some kind of abortion route, then I would not support them. But if they did go through with the pregnancy and had the baby, then I would be with them and would support them together with many other people. An abortion is nothing more than being completely selfish for your own sinful acts. I would just deeply encourage them to go through with the pregnancy, to take the responsibility. I would tell them to trust God and to re-evaluate their own life and actions. I would tell them that they need to take on the responsibility of having the baby which means to think about the baby – what would be helpful, what would be harmful?'

Whitney Evans, 20

I know that some of the girls, or couples reading this might really like the idea of having a cute little baby to look after. Some people think having a baby will help them feel loved and accepted because they think a baby will love them even if no one else will. Remember that no human can ever make us feel fully whole or loved, only God can do that. **WE SHOULD NEVER CREATE A NEW PERSON JUST TO FULFIL OUR OWN NEEDS**. Also, remember that cute little bundle will soon grow up to be a toddler needing constant attention and entertainment. If you feel like you really want a baby, please talk to someone you can trust about it. You could chat to a youth leader or perhaps an older friend who has children. They will be able to tell you what it's really like and help you make good decisions.

Worried you might be pregnant?

If you are worried that you are pregnant, take a pregnancy test – you can pick one up from a chemist for about £10. If you are pregnant, the best thing you can do is tell someone. It might seem scary but it's better to let people know as soon as possible so they can help and support you during this time. I promise people won't react as badly as you expect. If you can't talk to your parents talk to a youth leader or a friend who can give you good trustworthy advice.

ReactionReactionReactionReaction

CIRCLE:

TICK:

Total rubbish ☐   Not sure ☐   Worth thinking about ☐   Genius ☐

FILL:

....

....

....

....

....

Name: **Christian Alec**

Age: **13**

Town: **Jerusalem, Israel**

Who would win out of a fight between Batman, Spiderman and Superman?

Superman would win. Spiderman would run away. Batman would get burned in two seconds flat.

What is your catchphrase? **'High five for no reason . . .' (and then give them a high five).**

What do you think is strange about girls?

They all go to the bathroom together. Weird.

Advice about relationships?

Don't get into relationships too young. One time this girl told me that God had said to her that she was supposed to spend the rest of her life with me. If you think God has told you that and you're not over the age of 18, then it might not be from God.

How far is too far?

Stay away from the evil things a young person like you typically wants to do. Do your best to live right and to have faith, love and peace, together with others who trust in the Lord with pure hearts.

(2 Timothy 2:22)

4

First up

Now that we've found out what the Bible says about sex, and looked at reasons why it's best to keep sex for marriage, the obvious next question is, 'How far can we go then?' Is kissing OK? Is touching OK? Can we do everything but have sex? . . . The list of questions goes on. Throughout the years there have been many witty guidelines presented by youth leaders across the world. Our favourites include, 'Don't touch what you haven't got' (and no, touching nipples doesn't count as OK even though you both have them), 'Always stay vertical, not horizontal', and 'Don't do anything you wouldn't do if Jesus was watching'. These are great guidelines and we would recommend following them. However, we also think it would be good to take a step back and find out if asking 'How far is too far?' is really the right question.

Imagine if you were travelling with your girl/boyfriend along a busy motorway and the car broke down. The two of you end up walking on the edge of the road looking for help alongside speeding cars and lorries travelling at 70 miles per hour. Would you and your loved one walk as close as possible to the speeding vehicles, just because you could, or just to see how close you could get without getting hit? I doubt it. You'd both want the person you loved to stay as far away from danger as possible so they were guaranteed to be safe, rather than only just surviving. That's why **ASKING 'HOW FAR CAN WE GO?' IS THE WRONG QUESTION.** It's like asking, 'How close can we get to the speeding cars without getting run over?' By the time you learned the answer to that question, it would be too late as you'd have been run over. At the beginning of this section, we included a scripture that said, 'Stay away from the evil things a young person like you typically wants to do.' If someone was chasing you, you wouldn't attempt to stay close to them, you would run in the opposite direction, you would get as far away as possible.

When we ask the question, 'How far is too far?' it's like we are trying to see what we can get away with, or how close we can get to sex without getting in trouble. This is playing with fire. What we should be doing before marriage is running away in the opposite direction. We should be asking, 'How can I stay the purest possible?' or 'How much can I save for my husband/wife?' or 'How can I honour God most in this situation?' At the end of the day, God made sex as a great gift for you and your future spouse, he doesn't want for it to be spoiled, or for you to get hurt. When we turn against God with any sin, it breaks his heart, especially when we misuse a gift he made so carefully for us.

Where do you draw the line?

Bible Reading: 2 Timothy 2:20–22

Stay away from the evil things a young person like you typically wants to do. Do your best to live right.
(2 Timothy 2:22)

Have you ever thought, why do I have such strong sexual feelings if premarital sex is wrong? Maybe you've never asked that question out loud, but it might have danced through your mind. Don't you sometimes wonder why God made your desire for sex so potent if you can't do anything with it right now? Is God playing some kind of joke on you?

ot at all. Say thanks that you have a strong desire for sex – but also realize that you might have many years ahead of you to keep that desire under control until marriage. Your sex-saturated culture doesn't make it easy. But remember: God has given you all the power you need to keep your sexual desires in line. Follow his advice in 2 Timothy 2:22.

'So if sex before marriage is wrong,' you might still wonder, 'how far can you go? I mean, how far is too far?' Most kids want someone to step up, draw a bold line, and say, 'OK, everything up to here is fine. But if you go past this point, you're out of God's will.' **IT SOUNDS NICE AND SIMPLE, BUT IT DOESN'T WORK THAT WAY.**

Actually, there are better questions to ask than, 'How far is too far?' Try three: 'What caring actions can I use to show my true feelings to my date?' 'What actions best express how much I care about my date at this point in our relationship?' 'What is honest, righteous, and best for where we are right now?' But at the same time, the Bible is clear about drawing a line when it says, 'Never wrong any of your fellow believers or cheat them' (1Thessalonians 4:6). We 'cheat' others by taking from them to fulfil our sexual desires. Here's how to avoid that.

First, realize when you start wanting what you can't have. It usually starts so slowly that you don't realize it's happening. But when you raise your own desires above what's right and spiritually healthy, you have crossed an important line.

Second, aim at applying the command to love one another. Learn to love the 1 Corinthians 13 way – selflessly seeking out God's best for the other person.

Third, recognize that physical affection between a guy and girl is exciting because God made it that way. And it's progressive – one stage naturally leads to the next. Setting your standards and drawing your 'lines' ahead of time will enable you to stand up in a situation that requires some serious resisting and keeps you from making a mistake you might later regret.

Josh McDowell, *Youth Devotions 2*, **Tyndale House, 2003**

Reaction Reaction Reaction Reaction

CIRCLE:

TICK:

Total rubbish ☐ Not sure ☐ Worth thinking about ☐ Genius ☐

FILL:

....

....

....

....

....

For the boys

Chip talks

Many of you probably already know that I used to be in a band called thebandwithnoname. The band has undergone several changes in our line-up over the years, and I've had the incredible opportunity of performing alongside some seriously talented godly men. People like Zulu . . .

I'll never forget something Zulu once said when we were ministering in a young offenders institute. It was an all male audience, and these tough lads just sat there with their arms crossed for the entire performance. Heaven forbid that they should actually display some form of enthusiasm and lose their street credibility. Anyway, Zulu was talking about the importance of respecting people of the opposite sex. He was trying to explain why Christians believe they should remain virgins until they're married. As you can probably imagine, this concept didn't go down too well to begin with. Honestly though, you have not lived until you've attempted to explain sexual purity to a bunch of hardened criminals.

But then Zulu tried a simple experiment. He asked, 'Put your hands up if you think it's OK to sleep around before you're married?' Hands went up all over the room. Then he said, 'OK, now answer this: **HOW MANY MEN DO YOU WANT YOUR WIFE TO HAVE SLEPT WITH BEFORE SHE MARRIES YOU?'** To our utter surprise, the answer was a unanimous 'NONE!' Zulu just stood there and let the reality of their own hypocrisy sink in. It was quite funny to watch, actually, as the penny dropped for each one of those young men. They began to nod at each other and smile at their own embarrassment. There was really no need for Zulu to say any more. He'd made his point.

The Bible says in 1 Timothy 5:2 that you should 'treat the younger women with respect like sisters'. This is probably the best advice anywhere in the Bible for young men wondering how far they should explore sexual intimacy outside of marriage. It proves that if we truly do respect the fine young ladies around us, then we'll treat them as sisters – not objects for our own sexual gratification. We should be willing to place their needs above ours, and even protect them from other young men who have impure motives.

It doesn't take a brain surgeon to see that girls are wired differently than boys. They're very emotional creatures. They crave lasting friendships and security. Despite the fact that some of them may appear tough on the outside, all girls are actually quite vulnerable and sensitive deep down. They deserve to be treated like princesses. Their hearts should be courted and won, not borrowed and broken.

Take a moment to seriously evaluate the way you treat girls at this crucial stage of your life. Do you treat them with respect? Do you keep your promises to them? **DO YOU STAND UP FOR THEM AND DEFEND THEIR HONOUR?** What about your thought life? Do you make polite conversation with girls while secretly undressing them in your head?

In Matthew 5:27,28, Jesus said, 'You have heard that it was said, "You must not commit adultery." But I tell you that if a man looks at a woman and wants to sin sexually with her, he has already committed that sin with her in his mind.' Pornography is a serious issue in today's world. It's more accessible than ever before, and people everywhere are getting caught in downward spirals of addiction to something that at its core is really just disrespect towards women. As young men, we need to pray for each other and even be willing to confess our faults to one another. It's important that we have accountability partners who can identify with our weaknesses and feel free to challenge us regularly. It might be embarrassing and humiliating to begin with, but in the long run it'll prove to be extremely worthwhile.

So in conclusion, next time you're about to thrust yourself headlong into a relationship with a girl – think before you act. What are *her* needs? Will you treat her like a sister? Are you promising something you can't follow through on? Are you winning her heart or just breaking it? Remember that some guy somewhere may just be treating your future wife the same way!

ReactionReactionReactionReaction

CIRCLE:

TICK:

Total rubbish ☐   Not sure ☐   Worth thinking about ☐   Genius ☐

FILL:

....

....

....

Name: **Lloyd Moore**

Age: **14**

Town: **Cheltenham (right next to where Greenbelt happens)**

Passions: **Music and sport**

Which team do you support?

Ospreys (rugby union)

How many girls (approx.) have you fancied in your whole life?

Seriously? Three

How long did you fancy them for (on average)?

About a year. Then we became friends.

What advice do you have for people who want to be friends, but feel pressured into being more than friends?

Be friends first, and if you really think you love them, take it further.

For the girls

Helen talks

First up girls, I just want to say that you are amazing. You are beautiful, you are made just the way God wanted you and you have so much worth. I want you to know that you are a child of God, a child of the King and that makes you a princess for the best, biggest King ever. So RESPECT yourself. Have confidence in yourself and in the God who made you. Don't ever feel like you have to do anything you don't want to in order to please someone else. If you are ever with a guy who doesn't respect and treat you like the princess you are, then move on. You are worth so much more. Don't ever think, 'Well, this might be my only chance', or 'What if no one else ever likes me?' The God who loves you, who made you and everyone else in the world, knows what you need and will provide it in his right time.

Of course, that said, as ladies we also need to respect the lads out there and behave in a way that is honouring to them. It wasn't until I got married and could really talk openly with a lad about sex, that I found out how visual they are. Now I know us girls might get a bit excited at the thought of the Diet Coke guy with his shirt off and all his muscles showing, but believe me that's nothing to how a good looking girl can affect the lads. I know that when girls dress, we are often dressing to please ourselves or impress other girls as much as showing off to lads. We're trying to fit in with fashion trends, or with what we see other women wearing or with what feels good, but girls, we need to be aware of the effect our wardrobe has on members of the opposite sex. If you go out in a tiny skin-tight skirt, or very low top, it is going to cause lots of guys to struggle with lustful thoughts. Think about it, boys are assaulted all the time with images of half naked (or even all naked) women, in magazines, on TV, on billboards. As women of God we should be going out of our way to make their lives easier, not harder. If you turn up at youth group or church showing off all your 'assets', you are likely to make someone in the room struggle with lust or impure thoughts.

Now I'm not saying you should dress like a frump and go out of your way to be unattractive, not at all. **GOD MADE YOU BEAUTIFUL SO CELEBRATE IT**, but do it in a sensitive way. The media sells us the lie that we are only beautiful if we are sexy, we are only sexy if we show off lots of skin. That's just not true, you can look beautiful and attractive and be respectful of the lads in the room. Let's also be honest about our motives: if you are dressing to attract attention because it makes you feel good then you need to bring those feelings of insecurity to God. He made you just the way you are and he loves you just the way you are. God has a plan for you and you don't need to flaunt your body to make it happen.

Here's another thing, I know it can be quite easy for us ladies to flirt and lead lads on if we're in the mood. Maybe we just want someone to snog for the night, or we just want some attention. **DON'T DO IT**. Despite their tough exteriors many lads are very sensitive and can sometimes get emotionally involved even quicker than we can. So don't lead them on. If you are intending to stay pure and save yourself for marriage then don't push all the buttons that are going to make lads want to go further. Don't mess around with people's emotions if you aren't really interested in having a proper relationship with them. As girls of God we should always be trying to live to the highest standard and that includes how we treat lads. If you treat others with respect and dignity, chances are you will get the same treatment back.

So have a think about the way you treat and react to members of the opposite sex. If it's not been the best, then say sorry to God and ask him to help you change. You deserve the best, the best from sex, which means doing it in God's timing, and the best from relationships and marriage. Waiting for the right person might not always feel good but it's definitely worth it.

ReactionReactionReactionReaction

CIRCLE:

TICK:

Total rubbish ☐   Not sure ☐   Worth thinking about ☐   Genius ☐

FILL:

....

....

....

Taking control

Bible reading: Proverbs 6:24–29

Such a woman might be beautiful, but don't let that beauty tempt you. Don't let her eyes capture you.
(Proverbs 6:25)

'Before I became a Christian, I messed around sexually,' Tyler admitted. 'I expected trusting Christ would make all my wrong desires vanish. So far it hasn't worked that way. I'm reading my Bible, praying, and getting close to new Christian friends. But what else can I do?'

Just keeping in step with God won't automatically guarantee your bouts with lust will disappear. The important point is how you deal with them. Here are some practical principles to help you handle sexual temptations:

- Your body is a spiritual battlefield. Get used to the idea that the war will continue until Christ returns. There will always be a struggle.

- Take responsibility for your actions. What might trip you up is the rampant idea that sexual urges are beyond your control. God created you in his image with infinite value and dignity – and with the ability to make moral, righteous decisions and abide by them. Most of the time people land in bad situations because they dive into them.

- Control your thought life, because that is where lust begins. There is no way to put a lid on sinful thoughts outside of filling your mind with God's Word. Here are some scriptures that can help: Psalm 51; Proverbs 6:27,28; Romans 6:12–14; 1 Corinthians 6:9–11 and 10:13; James 1:12 and 4:7; and 1 John 4:4.

- Choose your friends carefully. Make sure your closest chums are people who help you, not who make it harder for you to handle temptation. Right friends can help you make right choices.

- Don't get overconfident about lust. But don't get overly fearful either. You put yourself in danger at either extreme.

- Admit your struggles and sins to God as well as to another Christian you trust. Talking openly can protect you from fooling yourself.

- When you see or meet someone who brings lustful thoughts to mind, force yourself to look in that person's face and eyes. Changing where you aim your eyes sounds trite but it helps you recognize and respond to the real person that is there and not just to the body that person is living in.

These truths have been used by thousands of students like you. Combining these weapons with a steady stream of prayer will keep your mind and body safe.

Josh McDowell, *Youth Devotions 2*, Tyndale House, 2003

ReactionReactionReactionReaction

CIRCLE:

☺ ☹ 😐 😯 😌 😲

TICK:

Total rubbish ☐ Not sure ☐ Worth thinking about ☐ Genius ☐

FILL:

....

....

Hidden pearls

'It must be very difficult for young people these days not to have sex before marriage. I would recommend that you steer clear of getting in circumstances where it can happen. If you go on holiday, don't stay in the same room. It is difficult though . . . we're all human beings. The Bible makes it clear how difficult it is, even David had problems.'

Reality Check

SETTING BOUNDARIES

If you wait till you are 'in the moment' to set boundaries then you are likely to do something you might regret.

Practical

Timing – Decide how long you think it is wise to spend alone in a room or house with your boy/girlfriend when you don't have anything to do.

20 minutes   40 minutes   1 hour   2 hours

Other ....

Curfew – Decide what time is too late for you to be alone with your boy/girlfriend in their home.

10pm   11pm   12am   1am

Other ....

Place – Write down some places where you think it would be unhelpful for you to be with your boy/girlfriend alone. For example, in their bedroom with the door closed.

....
....

Activity – Write down some activities that you will avoid doing with your boy/girlfriend because they might cause you to struggle. For example, watching 18 rated movies with sexual content.

....
....
....
....

STOP

Thought life

All actions begin with thoughts. Write down some resolutions about how you will keep your thought life pure. For example, not watching 18 rated movies, or deciding to put a net nanny on your PC so you can't view certain websites.

....

....

....

....

Emotional

Dating and being physical with lots of different people will lead to emotional hurt and pain. Make some resolutions to avoid relationships that aren't going anywhere and which could damage you emotionally.

Before I choose to start a relationship with someone I will: (tick as many as you want and add your own)

- Get to know them as a friend for as long as possible

- Find out as much as possible about them from other people

- Find out about their dating habits – are they a serial dater, or are they really interested in me?

- Take it slowly and decide if there is any future in the relationship before giving my whole heart to the person

- Get out of the relationship as soon as possible if it's not going anywhere

- ....

- ....

- ....

- ....

Physical

Make some decisions about your physical boundaries. Remember that going as far as you possibly can is not really honouring to God, yourself or your partner. We know some people who took this so seriously that they didn't even kiss until they were married! Write your own guidelines on how far you will go physically. For example, I won't lie down with someone of the opposite sex.

....

....

....

....

Accountability

Write down the name of someone who will hold you accountable and check if you are sticking to all these things.

Name: ....

When will you meet up with them and show them this list of resolutions?

This week

Next week

In two weeks' time

Other ....

How often will you meet up with them to make sure you are still on the right track?

Weekly

Fortnightly

Monthly

Other ....

Well done for thinking in advance about dating and sex and for making decisions about how you will stay pure for marriage. Sign below as a declaration that you will try to stick to everything you have written above.

Signed ....

Date ....

Name: **Abbi Denney**

Age: **19**

Town: **Bracknell**

Current status: **Youth Worker on a year out: taking assemblies, mentoring**

Tell us about your favourite Christmas you ever had.

I celebrated it with my boyfriend who celebrates Christmas as it should be done. We had a family roast dinner, and we opened presents, it was brilliant.

How do you want to do church in the future?

I want to do it out on the street. My vision is to have it on a bandstand in the centre of town with decent worship and a great witness.

Are you in a serious relationship?

Yes, my first one. I met him on thebandwithnoname's Revolution Tour! We chatted over the Internet for about a year and then we decided that we liked each other. But right now it's mostly a long-distance relationship.

Did he just say that?

God knows it,

because he knows our deepest secrets.

(Psalm 44:21)

5

First up

While we were compiling material for this book, we came across a lot of taboo issues that we didn't expect to see covered in Christian books. It makes total sense that these books are out there, and it's really important to get good information on subjects we sometimes don't feel able to talk about. This lesson will look at homosexuality, pornography, masturbation and sexual abuse. Undoubtedly, these things were issues when we were teenagers, but you guys definitely have to deal with them much more than we ever did. The invention of the Internet (it wasn't around when we were your age, and we're not even that old!) has meant that access to pornography is now extremely easy; in fact it's often hard to avoid. Homosexuality is now a much more accepted lifestyle than it was when we were teenagers, and the Christian viewpoint of sex being shared between a man and a woman within marriage is reacted against with increasing hostility. Unfortunately, there has been a huge rise in incidents of sexual abuse and it is something we now hear about often on the news.

It is a time when we need to know and stand up for what we believe as Christians, but not in a religious, 'we know better than you' kind of way. You guys have an amazing opportunity to show love to people of all colours, beliefs and sexual persuasions. You have the chance to reach out and support people who struggle with sexual issues or have been abused. In the past, Christians have been judgemental or just plain ignorant about many of these issues – they were too taboo to talk about even if they did go on behind closed doors. As young people living in a society where almost anything can be discussed openly, you have a real opportunity to be there for people in a way the church may have failed to be in the past. You also have the greatest challenge and task which is to stay pure – and that includes when you are home alone as much as when you are with another person. Rise to the challenge.

Homosexuality

One issue that has and continues to create loads of attention in the newspapers is what Christians think about being gay. Christians have been called 'gay bashers' and many people assume that God and Christians hate gays. Many gays speak about being rejected by churches, so what's going on? What does God think about being gay? Can you love God and fancy someone of the same sex? Here is the story of one guy who is gay and a Christian.

'I won't say I have always known, because I don't think I have! When I was in Year 9, I knew I was attracted to guys but knew what the Christian view on that was, so therefore thought it couldn't possibly be true. I kept denying it to myself until Year 12. At this point I decided that it was the way I felt and I couldn't really do anything about it. I still kept quiet about it though and invented a girl I fancied, to get people off the scent. Many people picked on me at school during Years 10 and 11, especially. I often got called all the names under the sun that related to being gay . . . They just thought it was funny to pick on me. And, to be honest I didn't fully know then either.

'How did I realize? Well I guess I just had feelings for guys that I knew I should be having for girls! I do believe, however, whatever people say, that it is very much a nurture thing. [Something about your environment that influences you.] The cause of this nurture is different for many people. I believe for me it was growing up with mainly female friends, the way they talked and thought really influenced me. I also think the names I was called at school were a factor. If you hear something long enough, you start to believe it. I find it very difficult to relate to guys [as just mates] and have never really had the male-male friendships that I think are so important. I was always getting rejected by guys. The longing for friendship developed into the wrong desires. Even now I really have to work at my male friendships.

'As time has gone on, life has got harder. Society has a certain level of expectation and if you don't meet that, people start to ask questions. Pretending to like girls when I was at school was relatively easy – but as life has gone on it's harder to pretend. The effort to 'lie' all the time just becomes a burden, but I know it has to be that way.

'I know what is right by God, and at times that is not a problem – I'm happy to follow God and live a single life. There are times, however, when it all seems so unfair and I wish I could just do what I like. Sometimes I do things I know I shouldn't but I never get very far. I always feel the guilt and have the 'God knowledge' of what is right and wrong . . . However hard I try, sometimes I know that I could never go my own way because I know the truth about God and it just doesn't fit.

'I get annoyed when I hear Christians debating the issue. Very rarely do I hear anything positive and/or helpful. On the one hand, you have Christians who think a gay lifestyle fits with the Bible (AS IF!). If I hear one more time, 'Nothing makes God happier, than when two people . . . any two people, join together in love!' I will scream!! I don't want to hear it fits because I know full well that it doesn't. People who say that are, in my opinion, trying to justify it to themselves. I can understand why, but they can't compromise the gospel just because it doesn't fit with how they feel! The other side of the argument is just as annoying – those Christians who think just because someone is gay they can't be a Christian. What version of the Bible says the gospel is for everyone but gay people? As I've already said, as I get older it is a lot harder to deal with. All your friends get into relationships and get married and you are left alone. Knowing that I am going to be a singleton for the rest of my life is not fantastic, but I have to believe God will give me strength to do it. It can be no other way. I try not to get angry with people who are so desperate for love that they ignore so many other things in life until they find someone. They need to learn, as I am having to, that happiness and belonging can be found in other things. I know it is not the same, but if God requires this, who am I to argue – look what he has done for me!

'Being a Christian through all this has both helped and hindered me. I know that if I wasn't a Christian, at times, I would have been so much happier. I could live the life I want. However, I know deep down that I won't find what I am looking for there. I know that this life is not all there is. And one day, when I get to heaven, I won't have to deal with this any more.

'Keeping it to myself is difficult. Sometimes I would like everyone to know and not have to constantly think about how I am acting and what I am saying. I long to be able to live in a society where it doesn't matter. However, I know life is not that simple. If I were to make it public knowledge, I would have to deal with people rejecting me for something I cannot help and would change if I could. I don't want to be going through this but I don't have any choice.'

Ems Hancock and Ian Henderson, *Sorted?*, Authentic, 2004

ReactionReactionReactionReaction

CIRCLE:

TICK:

Total rubbish ☐   Not sure ☐   Worth thinking about ☐   Genius ☐

FILL:

....

....

....

....

....

Masturbation

Let's start with a dictionary definition. Masturbation, according to www.dictionary.com, is defined as:

n. Excitation of one's own or another's genital organs, usually to orgasm, by manual contact or means other than sexual intercourse.

(American Heritage Dictionary)

That sounds very medical doesn't it?! If you read between the technical talk, what it's saying is that masturbation is bringing yourself, or another person, to climax or orgasm without having full-on sex. Usually, when people refer to masturbation they are talking about doing it solo and not involving anyone else. However, you can also stimulate someone else without having full-on sex with them and this would technically be masturbation. So now we are all clear on what it is, the big question is whether it's OK or not, right?

The mainstream, non-Christian view seems to be that masturbation is absolutely fine. Many magazines encourage teenagers to do it so that they will know what it's like, and some even promise that you will enjoy real sex more if you have practised masturbating loads before you do it. The Bible doesn't specifically say, 'thou shalt not masturbate', but the general Christian stance is that masturbation should be avoided. Some of the reasons for this are that masturbating is probably going to make it harder to stay away from sex outside of marriage, it will make it harder to stay away from lust and it can be very addictive. Although the Bible doesn't talk specifically about masturbation, it does have a lot to say about not looking on others with lust or desire (Job 31:1–3), about staying pure (2 Corinthians 7:1) and not living the way the world lives (2 Corinthians 10:3–5).

You might think that masturbation is harmless fun and that it doesn't hurt anyone. **AT LEAST YOU AREN'T SLEEPING AROUND, RIGHT?** Of course, masturbation has less consequences than sex with another person but it awakens desires and feelings in you that will have to be controlled if you are committed to sexual purity. If you are committed to not having sex before marriage, then you should be running away from temptation and making life as easy as possible for yourself, rather than seeing how close you can get to the line. By masturbating, you are experiencing a form of sexual satisfaction that will not last. It will always create the need for more. God created sex to be an intimate and fulfilling experience between two people.

MASTURBATION IS A CHEAP COPY OF THE REAL THING and so will ultimately end in a lack of true satisfaction and the need for more. It can often be a slippery addictive slope full of guilt that ends up with full sex, either in your mind, or for real, with another person.

Some people argue that they can masturbate without thinking lustfully of another person, but even if it starts out that way, like any kind of addiction, it can be hard to maintain. Often you will find yourself needing more and more to satisfy yourself. The next chapter talks about pornography, which is often involved in masturbation, especially for boys. Jesus said that even by thinking lustfully about someone you had committed adultery in your heart – see Matthew 5:28. Hardcore!

This might all seem a bit harsh, but think about it. If you have committed to a diet and you know that there is a bit of chocolate cake in the fridge, where is the best place for you? Probably outside the house having fun with your mates somewhere, not sitting with the fridge door wide open stroking the icing! Which scenario is going to help you best avoid the temptation? The good news is that God isn't a cruel evil tyrant who wants to make it difficult for you to keep his laws. He is a loving father who wants the best for you. The Bible says, 'The only temptations that you have are the same temptations that all people have. But you can trust God. He will not let you be tempted more than you can bear. But when you are tempted, God will also give you a way to escape that temptation. Then you will be able to endure it' (1 Corinthians 10:13). Also, 'Jesus, our high priest, is able to understand our weaknesses. When Jesus lived on earth, he was tempted in every way. He was tempted in the same ways we are tempted, but he never sinned. With Jesus as our high priest, we can feel free to come before God's throne where there is grace. There we receive mercy and kindness to help us when we need it' (Hebrews 4:15,16).

It may not seem like the kind of thing you can talk to God about, but if you are struggling with masturbation then tell him. Pray about it, be honest and ask the Holy Spirit to help you. Like any other temptation, another good way to deal with it is to be accountable to someone else. Many things are a lot less tempting when you know someone you respect is going to ask you if you have done them! It might seem impossibly hard to talk about it, but **YOU AREN'T THE ONLY ONE WHO HAS EVER STRUGGLED.** If you chat to someone older and wiser and ask them to keep you accountable they will understand. They probably had the same struggles you do.

ReactionReactionReactionReaction

CIRCLE:

☺ ☹ 😐 ❗ 😌 😮

TICK:

Total rubbish ☐   Not sure ☐   Worth thinking about ☐   Genius ☐

FILL:

....
....
....
....
....

Is masturbation OK?

There are a lot of myths around masturbation, such as it makes you blind! These are totally untrue. Masturbation can temporarily relieve sexual tension and is sometimes successfully used by therapists to help patients with low sexual desire.

H owever, on the minus side of the equation, it can often leave you feeling inexplicably unfulfilled and often guilty, at least initially. Sex experts often struggle to explain this but I think it has its roots in the meaning of sex.

Sex is, first and foremost, a means of communication and not just recreation. At its very best, sex communicates the message 'I love you and I am totally yours.' In solo sex, of course, this message can be an expression of self-centredness, rather than self-giving love.

If hours and hours of time are taken up with masturbating (as is often the case for boys and sometimes now for girls, too), this can cause problems. Frequent masturbation is invariably linked with using pornography and this is potentially harmful in the long term as it depersonalizes sex, separating it from a real and meaningful relationship. Pornography is all about sexual pleasure without responsibility or commitment. Unfortunately, **WHAT YOU FEED YOUR MIND ON HAS A NASTY HABIT OF FEEDING ON YOU EVENTUALLY.**

Masturbation of, or by, another person is a form of sexual climaxing and it can certainly run the risk of passing on sexually transmitted infection. Pregnancy, though, is highly unlikely, unless you move on to penetrative intercourse, which can easily happen in the heat of the moment.

Trevor Stammers and Tim Doak, *Saving Sex*, Authentic, 2006

ReactionReactionReactionReaction

CIRCLE:

TICK:

Total rubbish ☐   Not sure ☐   Worth thinking about ☐   Genius ☐

FILL:

....

....

....

....

....

....

....

Pornography

At the risk of sounding like the dad from *American Pie*, we are going to talk about pornography. Unlike him, we are going to assume that you know what it is and what it's like. At some point you might have seen a porn magazine, website, or something on TV. You might look at porn regularly or maybe you live with someone who looks at a lot of porn.

Pornography acts like a drug. You may start looking at or reading something every now and then but the desire grows and, like a drug, it becomes difficult to ignore. Also, as with drugs, you can become tolerant. A drug user has to take more and more drugs to get the same feelings. With porn, something that used to excite you doesn't any more, so you are drawn deeper and deeper into its dark world. Porn is a liar. It gives a false and unhelpful view of the opposite sex and of making love. It will mess with and pollute your mind, which is something the Bible tells us to avoid.

However, if you are a Christian who struggles with pornography, you already know that it is harmful and not what God wants. You may hate how weak you can be, and carry a lot of guilt. Here are some simple tips:

Make it difficult to get hold of: This might sound obvious but get rid of anything you know you go back to: videos, books or magazines. If you haven't got one, set up a 'nanny' programme on your computer. This will stop you looking at adult sites.

Bring it into the open: Much of the power that pornography has over people is that it is used in secret. Bringing it into the open means telling someone your secret. This is called being accountable. Once you've talked to someone you can trust and they have prayed with you, promise to tell them every time you use porn. It is important you find someone who you know won't judge you but will pray with you and help you. However, it's also important that you find someone who you don't want to disappoint. The thought of having to tell someone you respect and trust might help you not to click on that website or open that mag' in the first place.

Search your heart: If pornography has become a habit, you will need to ask God to 'break the control' you have given porn in your life. As you do this (often this is best to do with someone else), ask God if you have other areas in your life which you need to repent of. Sinful attitudes and actions can grow from your involvement with porn (it's not just what you do late at night). As well as these things, God may show you a connection between something that has happened in your life that you need healing from. You might find it difficult to see what impact that has on your struggle with porn. But the Holy Spirit knows your heart. Spend time asking and listening to what he has to say.

Know forgiveness: The devil will tell you that someone who has seen the things you have seen or done what you have done is unforgivable. This is a lie. God loves to forgive you. He's your dad, he loves sorting you out.

Ems Hancock and Ian Henderson, *Sorted?*, Authentic, 2004

ReactionReactionReactionReaction

CIRCLE:

TICK:

Total rubbish ☐   Not sure ☐   Worth thinking about ☐   Genius ☐

FILL:

....

....

....

....

....

Your escape route

Proverbs 7:21–27

Don't let your heart lead you to an evil woman like that. Don't go where she wants to lead you.
(Proverbs 7:25)

It's no secret that sexual desires are potent. And like a young guy named Mitch found out, they can blow up on you if you aren't careful. That's just as true for girls as it is for guys.

Mitch's first mistake was deciding to satisfy his growing curiosity about sex in the same ways most of his friends were – by staring at all the sex magazines and videos he could get his hands on. He told himself it was OK because he would find out everything he wanted to know about women and sexuality, and his curiosity would then be satisfied. Since he wasn't fooling around himself, he thought he could be wise about sex without sinning.

But the only thing Mitch accomplished was filling his mind with **TWISTED IDEAS ABOUT SEX**. When he dated, he could hardly help imagining trying out what he had read about and seen. Instead of satisfying his curiosity, the 'information' he stored in his brain from magazines and movies produced huge battles with guilt.

There's hardly anyone who can claim to be out of reach of the temptations Mitch faced. How can you avoid getting snagged in the same snare?

First, promise yourself that no matter what you ever feel or do sexually, you will find someone – like a parent or a mature friend – to talk to when you need information or just need to talk. Big hint: find someone older than your friends, who are going through the same pains you are.

Second, get out your Bible and concordance – or a Bible software program –

and search under all the headlines like 'lust', 'passions', and 'sexual immorality'. Write out what you learn on note cards and read through these cards at least once a week – more often if your feelings about sex are out of line with how God sees the subject.

Third, write a private note to yourself. On the left half of the page, spell out the specific standards and commitments you want to keep and why. On the right side write down the best plan you can think of for escaping when you are tempted to sin sexually. You can't count on having clear, creative thinking when you're in the middle of intense temptation. That's nearly impossible. But it's amazing how God will remind you of what you wrote down earlier as a way of escape.

Guys and girls choose all kinds of ways to quench their curiosity about sex. Friends may pressure you to join them in actions that mess up your mind – and your body. But by choosing your own, better way to handle sexual pressure, you gain genuine independence. You grab hold of your God-given freedom to choose.

Josh McDowell, *Youth Devotions 2*, Tyndale House, 2003

ReactionReactionReactionReaction

CIRCLE:

TICK:

Total rubbish ☐   Not sure ☐   Worth thinking about ☐   Genius ☐

FILL:

....
....
....
....
....

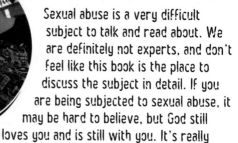

Sexual abuse is a very difficult subject to talk and read about. We are definitely not experts, and don't feel like this book is the place to discuss the subject in detail. If you are being subjected to sexual abuse, it may be hard to believe, but God still loves you and is still with you. It's really important that you talk to someone about your situation. It is not your fault and it is not what you deserve. The following extracts are just to help give a bit of advice but please talk to someone you know, or call 'Childline' or 'Samaritans' or check out books that can give you more help and information.

sexual harm

It may be helpful to list what we mean by sexual harm:

- If someone is kissing you when you don't want them to.
- If someone is touching you sexually or physically in an unwanted way.
- If someone is making you touch them sexually.
- If someone is constantly talking to you in a sexual way telling you what they want to do to you.
- If someone is forcing you to watch sexual acts.
- If someone is wanting to photograph or video you naked or doing anything sexual.

All these things are forms of sexual abuse. Harm of this sort is against the law. People can be prosecuted for their involvement in harming anyone in this way.

There may be someone at home, or someone that you know who is abusing you sexually. Someone you should be able to trust may be letting you down in a way that confuses you and makes you feel ashamed or scared. It may be as 'innocent' as holding you and cuddling you, but it may not stay that way and it already makes you feel uncomfortable. You know what this means and you are finding this hard to read, but please carry on. There are some young people and adults who for all sorts of reasons regularly seek to sexually abuse others. They probably will not even be able to see it as such. They would be shocked to be labelled as an 'abuser'. But that is what they are. They may be using you for physical or sexual contact that is unwanted by you and that you feel is totally inappropriate. But it makes you feel helpless and afraid. You have lived with it so far and you think you are OK, so you just let it continue. You may not know what else to do.

Why me?

If someone you know is touching you sexually or asking you to perform any act that you are uncomfortable with, you need to know that this is never right. It is also not your fault. No young person should be forced to do anything of a sexual nature that they are uncomfortable with. Don't be fooled into thinking that it has to continue or that it's somehow due to something you have done. Sexual abuse is very rarely caused by anything that you as a young person have done or said – other than the fact that you might be vulnerable. You may even think that you are not attractive and can't understand what draws this person to you. Don't be fooled into this lie.

You also need to know that what is happening to you is not because of God's anger towards you or because there is something wrong with you. If anyone has told you that, please know that this is both unhelpful and untrue.

The reason for abuse is never clear-cut. All we can say is that because we live in a world where people have the power to hurt as well as to heal, some people choose hurt. It's not fair and certainly not easy to live with, but it's not because of you that they do it. They are very damaged people who seek to damage others.

The future

One of the most important things for us to tell you is that there is hope for you. There is a future for you. Many of the abusive things that happen to young people happen in secret. Even really caring and loving parents may not know if someone they trust and know is abusing you. This means that it could carry on for longer. Whilst it is very hard, you may be the key to unlocking the problem. It may be time for you to try to end what is happening to you.

Here are some things that people who have been abused have done to begin helping themselves:

- **Admit that abuse is happening.**
- **Admit that it's not good and needs to stop.**
- **Admit that it's not your fault.**
- **Tell someone you trust who can talk and pray with you.**
- **Get some help – maybe from a trained professional (e.g. a school or college tutor, a counsellor or social worker).**
- **Meet up with others who have had the same experience.**

Ems Hancock and Ian Henderson, *Sorted?*, Authentic, 2004

ReactionReactionReactionReaction

CIRCLE:

TICK:

Total rubbish ☐   Not sure ☐   Worth thinking about ☐   Genius ☐

FILL:

....
....
....
....
....

Rape

Helen talks

Rape is when someone makes you have sex against your will. Sexual abuse, which we have just learned about, often happens when someone older abuses someone much younger, but many people are raped by people close to their own age. Sometimes this can happen at parties or get-togethers where there is drinking and/or drug-taking so people's defences are down. If you have ever been in a situation where you said no to sex and it happened anyway, whether you were drunk, sober or high, and whether you had been flirting or not, it is still abuse. You always have the right to say no at any point and you should never be made to feel like it was your fault. If you have been forced into a sexual situation that you did not want, even if you initially encouraged it, or were too out of it to realize what was going on at the time, then please seek help. There are rape counselling centres or phone lines in most areas or you can find advice on the Internet or talk to a trusted friend or counsellor. Don't suffer in silence. Often people are raped by people they know, perhaps someone from school, a friend's older brother or sister or some other acquaintance. This can make it even harder to deal with, especially if you are made to feel like you brought it upon yourself. However, it is really important that you get help. You may feel that you need to make a report to the police or you may not want to do this. It is your choice, but if you do want to press charges, having a medical examination as soon as possible will help your case. If you have been raped it is advisable to have a medical examination to check for any injuries, STDs or pregnancy, too.

Always remember that any kind of sexual abuse or rape is not your fault and that it will have had an emotional impact on you as well as a physical one. Getting help as soon as possible will help you deal with this emotional impact and make sure that you can be healed from the hurts you have suffered.

Obviously, avoidance is always better than cure, so try to avoid dangerous situations. If you are out drinking make sure someone knows where you are and who you are with. Make sure you have a lift home. Avoid going into situations where you will be alone with someone who could hurt you. Stay in control of your senses by not getting drunk or taking drugs, this will greatly increase your chances of avoiding dangerous situations. Always make sure you are looking out for yourself and your friends.

Second chances

Even if your sins are as dark as red dye, that stain can be removed and you will be as pure as wool that is as white as snow.

(Isaiah 1:18)

6

First up

So here we are at the last chapter of this book on sexuality. Hopefully, you have learned a lot more about what the Bible has to say about it. We've looked at how to deal with relationships, why God says it's important to wait until marriage for sex, how far you should go sexually before marriage and we've just looked at lots of subjects that are sometimes not discussed in church. We hope this book has helped you get a clearer image of why God says the things he does about sex and about how much he loves you and has a great plan for your life. He created sex as an amazing gift for us and when we use it properly it will bless us and God.

We know that there will be some of you reading this who have already had sex, or already gone further sexually than you think is right. There may be people who have been abused sexually and feel worthless and angry that their innocence has been taken from them. There may be others who felt pressured into having sex and now regret having done it, or perhaps you just got caught up in the moment and didn't stop until it was too late. We don't want to kid you that sexual sin has no consequences and that there may not be any effect in your life but we do want to tell you that there is forgiveness. Sexual sin is not the unforgivable sin – if we come to God and say sorry for anything we have done he will forgive us and wipe the slate clean. In Psalm 103:12 it says, 'and he has taken our sins as far away from us as the east is from the west'. Think about it. That is really, really far.

A lot of times when the Bible tells us to say sorry, it uses the word 'repent' – this means saying sorry, but it also means turning away from your sin. When you look at the original language the word was written in, it actually means to make a complete turn and go in the opposite direction! It's not enough just to say sorry and then carry on doing things you know are wrong, we need to say sorry and start to walk in a different direction.

As you read through this chapter, take time to say sorry to God and think about how you are going to walk in the opposite direction. Look back at the 'Reality check' where you planned what boundaries you were going to set to avoid giving in to sexual temptation. God wants the best for you, and it's not too late.

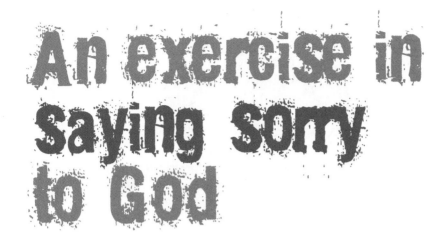

An exercise in saying sorry to God

Chip talks

Take some time now to read through Psalm 51 and ask God to forgive you for anything you have done sexually that you now think was wrong (this could include things you have thought and looked at as well as things you have done physically). This might not be the only time that you need to do this. Feel free to come back to this chapter in the Bible as often as you need to and let it help you find the words to tell God you're sorry. Remember, he is always there to listen to you and to forgive you.

Psalm 51:–17

> God, be merciful to me because of your faithful love.
> Because of your great compassion,
>   erase all the wrongs I have done.
> Scrub away my guilt. Wash me clean from my sin.
> I know I have done wrong. I remember my sin all the time.
> I did what you said is wrong.
> You are the one I have sinned against.
> I say this so that people will know that I am wrong
>   and you are right.
> What you decided is fair.
> I was born to do wrong,
>   a sinner before I left my mother's womb.
> You want me to be completely loyal,

so put true wisdom deep inside of me.
Remove my sin and make me pure.
Wash me until I am whiter than snow!
Let me hear sounds of joy and happiness again.
Let the bones you crushed be happy again.
Don't look at my sins. Erase them all.
God, create a pure heart in me,
  and make my spirit strong again.
Don't push me away or take your Holy Spirit from me.
Your help made me so happy. Give me that joy again.
Make my spirit strong and ready to obey you.
I will teach the guilty how you want them to live,
  and the sinners will come back to you.
God, spare me from the punishment of death.
My God, you are the one who saves me!
Let me sing about all the good things you do for me!
My Lord, I will open my mouth and sing your praises!
You don't really want sacrifices, or I would give them to you.
The sacrifice that God wants is a humble spirit.
God, you will not reject a person who comes to you
  with a broken heart, ready to obey.

Reaction Reaction Reaction Reaction

CIRCLE:

TICK:

Total rubbish ☐   Not sure ☐   Worth thinking about ☐   Genius ☐

FILL:

....

....

Name: Nick Cook

Age: 17

Town: High Wycombe, England

Current Status: Student in History, English, Psychology and Politics

Why politics?

Good question. It's important because the way countries are run and the way laws are passed affect everyone.

If you were asked to write a book, what would be the title?

'There's More'

What country do you have the biggest prayer burden for?

England and Israel, 50/50

What would you say to someone who is feeling extremely guilty for having had sex outside of marriage?

With guilt, you've got to let it go and give it to Jesus. He doesn't hate you for anything you've done. Don't feel condemned, feel convicted and then take it to Jesus and ask for forgiveness and let him take it away.

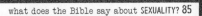

Forgiveness

chipK's mind

Most of the time my sister and I get along just fine. But when we were younger, we used to get into some terrible fights. I would call her names (my favourite was 'fat-hog-slob-pig'. Isn't that a great one? . . . um . . . I mean . . . isn't that terrible?), and she would respond by launching into a full-on physical assault. She knew I wasn't allowed to hit girls back so that was always her weapon of choice. One of our parents would inevitably break up the fight, telling us to apologize and forgive each other. Isn't it amazing how the words 'I forgive you' can be spoken through gritted teeth and squinted eyes, yet still sound totally convincing?

GOD'S LOVE FOR US IS UNCONDITIONAL. His anger towards our sin was completely used up on Jesus when he died in our place. When we admit the wrong stuff we've done and tell God how sorry we truly are, he will always forgive us. He chucks our sin as far away from us as the east is from the west. That's pretty far.

No matter how badly you've messed up, it's never too late to repent and ask God to forgive you.

He's a gracious Father who specializes in second-chance-giving, and his arms of love are wide open.

God's mind

Then Peter came to Jesus and asked, 'Lord, when someone won't stop doing wrong to me, how many times must I forgive them? Seven times?' Jesus answered, 'I tell you, you must forgive them more than seven times. You must continue to forgive them even if they do wrong to you seventy-seven times.'
(Matthew 18:21,22)

'When you are praying and you remember that you are angry with another person about something, forgive that person. Forgive them so that your Father in heaven will also forgive your sins.'
(Mark 11:25)

If we say that we have no sin, we are fooling ourselves, and the truth is not in us. But if we confess our sins, God will forgive us. We can trust God to do this. He always does what is right. He will make us clean from all the wrong things we have done.

(1 John 1:8,9)

He has taken our sins as far away from us as the east is from the west.

(Psalm 103:12)

His anger lasts for a little while, but then his kindness brings life. The night may be filled with tears, but in the morning we can sing for joy!

(Psalm 30:5)

Your mind

- **Can God forgive sexual sin?**

- **Why is it never easy to ask someone to forgive me?**

- **If someone who's offended me badly comes asking for forgiveness, why should I forgive them?**

- **Do I need to seek forgiveness today from God or anyone else? If so, who? And what for?**

Chip Kendall, *The Mind Of ChipK: Enter At Your Own Risk*, Authentic, 2005

Reaction ReactionReactionReaction

CIRCLE:

TICK:

Total rubbish ☐ Not sure ☐ Worth thinking about ☐ Genius ☐

FILL:

....

....

LAST UP

We started this book with a verse about learning to control our bodies and honouring God. This means waiting until you are ready and are in the right situation before making the commitment to have sex. We know that is so much easier said than done when the pressure is on to do what everyone else says you should do, but hopefully this book has helped you to understand why it's so important to wait. Use the information you've learned and the plans you've put in place and remember that God wants this for you too, it's not just your own battle. He will work with you on this if you ask him.

PRAY

Father, thank you for teaching me the truth about sex. Thank you that you designed me and know exactly what I need and what I don't need. Help me to set boundaries in my life to protect myself from doing things I might regret. Protect me from situations where I am likely to give in to temptation. Please give me wisdom and self-control as I conduct my relationships and help me to wait for the person you have chosen for me to marry.

In Jesus' name,

Amen.